Sorry I'm late. My hair won't start.

by Cathy Guisewite

Selected Cartoons from
A MOUTHFUL OF BREATH MINTS
AND NO ONE TO KISS
Volume 1

FAWCETT CREST • NEW YORK

Library of Congress Catalog Card Number: 83-71766

ISBN 0-449-20925-3

Manufactured in the United States of America

First Ballantine Books Edition: January 1986

10 9 8 7 6 5 4 3 2 1

PART OF ME DOESN'T EVEN CARE ABOUT VALENTINE'S DAY THIS YEAR... ANOTHER PART OF ME WANTS AN APARTMENT FULL OF CARDS AND FLOWERS...

PART OF ME THINKS VALENTINE'S DAY IS A CHEAP, COMMERCIALIZED EVENT... ANOTHER PART OF ME IS SCREAMING FOR PINK DOILIES AND POETRY...

PART OF ME DOESN'T NEED MY SELF-ESTEEM RAISED BY A VALENTINE... ANOTHER PART OF ME WOULD BEG AND GROVEL FOR ANYTHING WITH A HEART ON IT.

I'LL HAVE THE NACHOS FOR SIX.

SOMETIMES I GET THE FEEL-ING THAT I'M JUST WANDER-ING AROUND BETWEEN LADIES' ROOMS, ANDREA.

I GO TO WORK...I GO CHECK MY OUTFIT IN THE LADIES' ROOM...I GO TO A MEETING.....I GO CHECK MY HAIR IN THE LADIES' ROOM...

BEFORE, DURING AND AFTER EVERY EVENT OF MY LIFE, I MAKE THIS RITUALISTIC STOP IN THE LADIES' ROOM!

WELL, WHAT ARE YOU GOING TO DO TO CHANGE IT, CATHY?

I THINK MAYBE I'LL JUST STAY IN HERE.

MOM, WHAT ARE YOU GOING TO DO WITH 900 COPIES OF THE COMPANY NEWSLETTER THAT HAS MY PICTURE IN IT?

I'M GOING TO TAKE THEM DOWN TO THE SHOPPING MALL, SET UP A LITTLE BOOTH OUTSIDE THE HOT PRETZEL STAND AND FORCE PERFECT STRANGERS TO READ ABOUT YOU!

OH... I'M SORRY, MOM. I DIDN'T MEAN TO INSULT YOU. YOU CAN HAVE AS MANY COPIES AS YOU WANT.

WHAT DID SHE THINK I WAS GOING TO DO WITH THEM?

HOT PRETZEL

Read about my daughter

GUISEWITE

IF I WEAR THE OUTFIT I LOOK BEST IN ON MY FIRST DATE WITH THIS MAN, I WON'T HAVE ANYTHING TO WEAR IF I EVER GO OUT WITH HIM AGAIN.

THEN AGAIN, IF I DON'T WEAR WHAT I LOOK BEST IN, I'LL BE UNCOMFORTABLE ALL NIGHT, I'LL ACT WEIRD, AND THERE WON'T BE A SECOND DATE.

THEN AGAIN, IF I WEAR THE GREAT OUTFIT AND WE HAVE A WONDERFUL TIME, I'LL HAVE TO BUY A WHOLE NEW WARDROBE TO LIVE UP TO THE FIRST IMPRESSION I MADE.

I DECIDED TO STAY HOME AND WATCH TV.

EVERYWHERE YOU GO, THERE'S TOO MUCH STUFF TO BUY. I WENT TO THE DRUGSTORE FOR A TUBE OF TOOTHPASTE, I CAME OUT WITH A DINETTE SET.

I WENT TO THE GAS STATION FOR GAS, I CAME HOME WITH A 5-PIECE LUGGAGE ENSEMBLE.

I WENT TO THE CARD SHOP FOR A CARD, I CAME AWAY WITH AN ESPRESSO MACHINE. YOUR FATHER IS JUST GOING TO KILL ME.

WHERE **IS** DAD?

HE RAN OUT FOR A NEWSPAPER.

DID YOU HAVE A NICE WEEKEND, CATHY?

YES, MR. PINKLEY. I WENT TO THE SYMPHONY WITH A MAN I JUST MET.

HE OPENED MY EYES TO A WHOLE NEW WORLD AND MADE ME REALIZE HOW TRIVIAL AND MEANINGLESS MY BUSINESS PROBLEMS ARE.

THIS IS STUPID, BORING, DISGUSTING WORK, MR. PINKLEY. MY JOB MAKES ME SICK!!

...NEVER REPORT ON YOUR WEEKEND BEFORE YOU'VE HAD YOUR COFFEE.

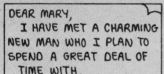

DAVID WENT BACK TO ST. LOUIS AND IRVING MOVED IN WITH HIS PARENTS. AT LEAST MY MOTHER WILL BE THRILLED.

IT WAS HORRIBLE TO SEE THEM LEAVE...BUT I JUST KEPT THINKING, "MOM IS GOING TO BE THRILLED".

SOME THINGS ARE WORTH GOING THROUGH IF ONLY BECAUSE YOU KNOW YOUR MOTHER WILL BE TOTALLY THRILLED!

...WHATEVER MAKES YOU HAPPY, DEAR.

WITH OUR NEW VIDEO TAPE RECORDER, WE WATCHED THE 6:00 NEWS AT 8:45. WE SAW YESTERDAY'S 3:00 MOVIE AT 5:20 TODAY.

WE SAW TUESDAY'S 8:00 SPECIAL AT 9:00 SATURDAY MORNING, AND THE 7:30 SUNDAY SYMPHONY DURING LUNCH ON WEDNESDAY.

MOM, THAT'S GREAT TO BE ABLE TO WATCH SHOWS WHEN YOU WANT! WHAT ARE YOU AND DAD GOING TO DO WITH ALL YOUR NEW SPARE TIME?

WE'RE GOING TO TRY TO FIGURE OUT WHAT DAY IT IS.

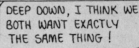

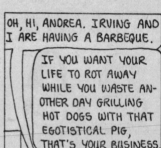

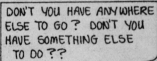

I READ A STORY ABOUT A WOMAN MY AGE WHO STARTED A COMPANY AND IS MAKING $200,000 A YEAR. I RAN HOME AND ATE A BOX OF DONUTS.

I TALKED TO A FRIEND WHO'S GROVELLING AROUND TRYING TO FIGURE OUT WHAT TO DO WITH HER LIFE. I CHARGED OVER TO MY OFFICE AND FINISHED 4 PROJECTS.

WHEN SALLY WAS MADE A VICE PRESIDENT, I ATE A CARTON OF COOL-WHIP... ...WHEN PAM GOT FIRED, I WROTE A BRILLIANT, 20-PAGE RESEARCH REPORT.

I'M RESPONDING TO ALL THE WRONG ROLE MODELS.

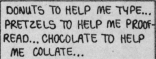

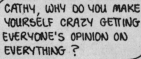